Break the Spell

Break the Spell

——— poems ———
Stacie Smith

SHANTI ARTS PUBLISHING
BRUNSWICK, MAINE

Break the Spell

Copyright © 2024 Stacie Smith

All Rights Reserved

Published by Shanti Arts Publishing

Designed by Shanti Arts Designs

Cover images: [front] Androlia (AI) / 731714517 / stock.adobe.com; [back] 성우 양 (AI) / 828350791 / stock.adobe.com

Shanti Arts LLC
193 Hillside Road
Brunswick, Maine 04011

shantiarts.com

Printed in the United States of America

ISBN: 978-1-962082-33-4 (softcover)

Library of Congress Control Number: 2024943727

*for Caroline Hunter and Lucinda Willoughby,
my maternal great-great-grandmothers*

ALSO BY STACIE SMITH

Open Burning

*Meanwhile the Earth:
Poems from Cougar Creek*

Real News

Second Sight (a collaboration
with June Campbell Rose)

Report from the Confluence

Trail to the Spring

What happens to humans happens to Earth.
What happens to Earth happens to humans.
The soul of the one is the soul of the other.

—Jules Cashford, *Gaia: Mother Goddess Earth*

Contents

ACKNOWLEDGMENTS / 15

PURE LIGHT DANCING
    IDEA / 18
    STARS AND CIRCUMSTANCE / 19
    START HERE / 20
    SILENT UNSEEN / 22
    WRITER'S BLOCK / 23
    PURE LIGHT DANCING / 24
    AMBERGRIS / 25
    AWAKE INTO DARKNESS / 26
    SCHEME OF THINGS / 27
    SYMBIOSIS / 28
    THE ANIMATE / 29
    SAND / 30
    MY BROTHER'S NEW POEM / 31
    SECRET / 32
    LAST NIGHT'S DREAM / 33
    ANOTHER DREAM / 34
    TWO MINDS / 35
    I WOKE UP WONDERING / 36
    ONE WORD / 37
    ONE MINUTE SNOW / 38

WAITING FOR RAIN
    WAITING FOR RAIN: SERIES II / 42
    LAHAINA / LITTLE CREEK / 43

BORAGE, TULSI, AND RUE / 44
LAPIS LAZULI / 45
FERAL CAT / 46
JENNIE'S GARDEN / 47
THE PRICE OF WINGS / 48
WHATEVER I SEE / 49
SUCH HAPPENINGS / 50
CAPE BLANCO / 51
ANY CLUE: WILDFIRE SERIES IV / 52
REPORT FROM QUAANAAQ / 53
PLAYA SERIES XIX / 54
COYOTE AND BUDDHA:
   COUGAR CREEK SERIES LXV / 55
HUNGRY ENOUGH / 56
DOWNHILL / 57
READY / 58
YACHATS: SERIES II / 59
LIVING PROOF / 60
WAITING FOR RAIN: SERIES III / 61

FLASH OF HOURS
BREAK THE SPELL / 64
MY JOB THESE DAYS / 65
BOOTSTRAPS: SERIES II / 66
BUCKET LIST / 67
MEMORY OF LIGHT / 68
FLASH OF HOURS / 69
ANHEDONIA / 70
HER HANDS / 71

MORE THAN MEETS / 72
HOW THE MOON MIGHT FEEL / 73
BIRTHDAY WISHES AT 77 / 74
BURNING OLD JOURNALS / 75
CROCUS / 76
THESE DAYS / 77
YOUR RIPENING / 78
THIRST / 79
OLD FACE / 80
WHAT ELSE I CAN DO / 81
FALLING / 82
SOLSTICE / 83

ABOUT THE AUTHOR / 85

ACKNOWLEDGMENTS

The author wishes to thank the editors of the following publications in which these poems first appeared:

Bellowing Ark: "Ambergris"

Real News (Shanti Arts, 2019): "What Else I Can Do"

Report from the Confluence (Shanti Arts, 2021): "Idea" and "Symbiosis"

Second Sight (Shanti Arts, 2020): "One Word" and "Falling"

PURE LIGHT DANCING

IDEA

A bright idea though voiceless at first
eventually finds a mind to reside in
just as a seed carried aloft by wind
sooner or later finds a place to land.

It seems there are madmen at the helm
but meanwhile in a parallel realm
a seed has landed on welcoming ground,
sending its roots down and down into darkness.

STARS AND CIRCUMSTANCE

The mystic you were born to be
is hiding now, trying to survive
these hunger times—your valor
under siege is taking refuge
in the neutral dark.

A seed rests hidden underground
while stars and circumstance align.
The mystic you were born to be
is hiding now but growing
slow and steady toward the light.

START HERE

Start here
where the map is marked
with a big bold X.

The next step
is a guess, a glimmer,
a hunch.

Between you and the treasure
lie many days and nights
of guessing.

Once upon a time
I encountered a crow whose eye—
I swear—looked directly into mine

and glinted like obsidian
sparking in me that old familiar lust
for better and different and more.

So I followed that crow
as it flew overhead
aiming west.

The shore it led me to
was unpeopled and vast.
I settled there—

no place else to go.
At the edge of the known world
I studied the art of poverty.

But oh yes—that map—
your job is to follow its clues.
They are yours alone.

Start now.
Each step is a guess
leading you home.

SILENT UNSEEN

The language of overlords
was coerced on my tongue
from the day I was born.
What's left of me yearns
to unlearn it—

to rewrite everything
unwrite any poem
that isn't in tune
with the silent unseen
that spawned us.

WRITER'S BLOCK

Start with one word
for instance *maybe*
or *someday*
or *beyond*

Any of these
can launch a poem
or a letter to a friend
or a song

so if you think
you can't get started
just pick a word
or better yet, two

like *hard rain*
or *long shot*
or *sweet tooth*
or *brighter days*

Be like a baby
learning to speak.
Go ahead—
try *anything*.

PURE LIGHT DANCING

In this realm of broken bridges,
old stories that once consoled
are forgotten; the story-tellers
have lost their tongues.

So where do I go from here?
Shall I reach out one last time
for anything that shines, anyone
who claims to know the way?
Or shall I stay here, solo,
in what remains of home,
turning the dog-eared pages
in the book of love?

Shall I head out toward the edge
of another world, or shall I make do,
here in the rubble of false refuge?

My forbears were looking for gold.
Once upon a time I was too, but
now the only thing that glitters
is the pure light of day dancing
on the little creek outside my door.

AMBERGRIS

Digging long and deep for gold
the miners grew thin and desperate
and mean.

Then the whalers came
hunting for oil and ambergris
only to find death by drowning.

If I were gold or any other precious thing
I would hide far away and I would pray:
don't discover me.

AWAKE INTO DARKNESS

In my dream I jumped
from a moving train,
dropped hard to ground
then rolled downhill
pulled as if by a magnet
toward a bright presence
that called my name.

I jolted awake into darkness,
sensations still thrumming
in my feet, my belly, my hands.
What was I fleeing?
What was I falling toward?

Eventually I slept again,
dreamless, until morning,
the light of day pulling me
back into this waking dream
where I straddle two realms
—inner and outer—
one in the same.

SCHEME OF THINGS

I was minding my own business
hunting chanterelles
when suddenly the forest swallowed me,
and everything I thought I knew
began to melt like honey stirred in tea—
I can't explain what happened next
but all at once the moment opened wide
to show me:

> *here is how to love the world:*
> *notice how the ease you seek*
> *is in the air you breathe—*
> *give your full attention*
> *to whatever comes along—*
> *a friend, a memory, a song—*
> *a spiderweb, a shell, a seed—*
> *meaning is encrypted there—*
> *the scheme of things reveals itself*
> *in little signals everywhere.*

SYMBIOSIS

Trees inhale my exhalations,
using what my blood unloads
into the bellows of my lungs—
a symbiosis I can't live without.

These little poems are just thoughts
conveyed by words that ride my breath—
these words become the exhalations
of my meaning-seeking mind.

Speech requires my exhalations;
another symbiosis I can't live without,
not happily at least; this human being
has a mind that needs to see, then say.

Thought alone is nothing, just as green
and growing things without the necessary
stuff to photosynthesize can't breathe.
Thought needs words and words need me.

THE ANIMATE

In sudden heat, the morning
dilates, amplifies, shimmers.
A bamboo chime clatters
in response to hot wind.

The human world is upside down.
Pundits tell me I should be afraid, but
I would rather spend what's left of me
learning how to live right side up.

I open a book of cryptic little poems—
they recalibrate my worried mind.
They say: *Here is what the world means—
just look—all around us the actual,
the animate, the kind, the transparent day.*

SAND
—in memory of William Stafford

I remember what my teacher said:
*in your own words try to say
what your own life is trying to mean.*

So here I sit on this cold dune
watching shadows move on my knee,
trying to say what my life is trying to mean.
With these beach grasses for company
I'll start—in my own words—by describing
the sand that holds me up:

At a glance, its color is nondescript—
a pale uniform gray. But up close
I see tiny grains of agate, garnet, jade,
mother of pearl, flecks of glistening black
whose provenance might have been
an undersea eruption long ago,
its fiery plume spewing molten flint
halfway to space where then as ash
it drifted in a dark cloud carried aloft
by stratospheric wind until eventually
it landed—here—where my hand rests
from trying to write words that say
what my life is trying to mean.

MY BROTHER'S NEW POEM

As a little boy my brother occupied
a private inner realm—surreal and vast—
where lambs and lions could be best of friends
where strange fantastic cities rose and fell
where shadow metamorphosed into luminosity.

Now a man, he offers up dispatches
from that zone—a kind and neutral place—
where human foibles dance themselves to death
or end in an embrace.

His newest poem is an open letter
to our fallen world where angels
search the battlefield for wounded saints
and demons—equal victims of reality—
a message from a caring heart
addressed to anyone who dares to read.

SECRET

I want to
share a secret
without saying it
aloud and so
I'll put it here
on this thin page
where it can hide
within the confines
of these lines and
as a little poem
hurt no feelings
—no harm done:

> I love the rain
> as much as I
> love anyone

LAST NIGHT'S DREAM

last night's dream:
a lifeboat full of snow
a switchback trail
a country store
a kindly woman
tending shop
telling me:

*your pilgrimage
is risky
but remember
other devotees
of mystery
surround you
on your way.*

*hungry wolves
will follow you.
step carefully.
the path
that leads you
to the object
of your prayers
is nothing
but a dream
telling you*
  wake up
  wake up
  wake up

ANOTHER DREAM

In my dreams I am able to do
numinous, amazing things—
walk barefoot on the ocean floor,
talk with a long-dead friend,
swim to Paris, see in the dark.

In my waking days I am able to do
mundane things—light a candle,
brew a cup of tea, feed the birds,
buy a stamp, write some words,
make soup.

Moving back and forth between
those realms of night and day
I try my best to stay afloat,
to be a steady friend, to be
a source of mirth and clarity

but sometimes life is way beyond
my mortal ken and there is nothing
I can do but close my eyes and fall into
another dream and hope to wake again
into this same old mystery.

TWO MINDS

During waking hours
my mind tends to business,
stays on task more or less,
keeps its ducks in a row
but in dreams it has a mind
of its own—I can't be sure
it's even me dreaming them:

> in a tidal pool two women
> with flowing white-gold hair
> teach a young girl how to float
>
> in a huge blue tent on stilts
> an old friend from long ago appears,
> sprouts wings then skates away
>
> a bright hawk swoops down
> and lands inches from my feet
> then tugs at my toes

Still awash in surreality I wake up
and watch my down-to-business mind
put on its shoes and go to work
sorting fact from fiction, this from that,
reality from dream, doing everything
within its ken to try to understand
what any of it means.

I WOKE UP WONDERING
   —*after seeing images from the Hubble Telescope*

I woke up wondering—
do our bodies replicate the universe
and if they do I wonder why
when everyone who's born will die.

Then I got up
and brewed some black rose tea
while looking out my window
at forsythia and daffodils
ablaze in ominously early bloom.

"Too soon!" I thought, "Too soon!"
and then turned on the daily news
too ponderous and too bizarre
to possibly be made
from the stuff of stars.

And so to antidote the news
I sat and sipped my tea
and opened up a book of poems
from the thirteenth century
and felt a sudden brightening—
Rumi! Perfect remedy!

ONE WORD

Despite all my casting and waiting
not one word has taken the bait
so I reel in my line and call it a day.
If a poem wants to come, it will.
Who am I anyway, to think a fish
would take my little hook?

Back home and hungry
I put a skillet on the stove.
Dreaming of rainbow trout
I crack an egg instead.
Nothing to be done.
The holy is everywhere.

ONE MINUTE SNOW

One minute snow,
ice rain the next
followed by rumors
of flood or fire.

The refuge I seek
is not a person
or a place.

This world is a poem.
It has a mind
of its own.
Read it.

WAITING FOR RAIN

WAITING FOR RAIN
Series II

A dwindling creek—small, bright, and clear—
runs thin but steady on its downhill course
in full compliance with the laws of gravity.
It does me good to sit and witness
alternating light and shadow dancing
on the surface of that tiny waterway.

I watch it moving low and slow
according to its own inherent knowing.
The world of man is a tangle of dread
but water shows me what to do—
meet obstacles as they appear
and keep on flowing.

LAHAINA / LITTLE CREEK

In my garden tiny pollinators
harvest nectar from the flowers
of oregano and mint and thyme.
Windchimes ring, the creek
is a trickling silver thread.

Meanwhile on an island far away
sudden devastation strikes, fueled
by hurricane and human folly,
wildfire devouring any object,
any living being in its path.

Mute in the face of what I see,
not knowing what on earth
to do or say, I can only offer up
this poem as a prayer
for the newly dead.

BORAGE, TULSI, AND RUE

Beyond my door lies mayhem's habitat.
Humanity lives there in its tangle of woe.
I have no solutions, nothing to offer
but what comes to me in dreams—
a spark, a hunch, a numinosity—
a possibility that there's a remedy
in learning how to put my mind aside
and listen to the wind for clues.

Two worlds—a man-made one,
another, green and thriving
in bejeweled minutia—
Gaia's wild intelligence at play—
let the chaos roll on without me.
I'm here to watch honeybees
taste the Borage, Tulsi, and Rue.
The Earth knows what to do.

LAPIS LAZULI

Just now a small blue dragonfly
flew from the back of my hand
where she'd rested briefly on her way—
her body the color of lapis lazuli—
glossy, with transparent wings
and eyes shining like jade beads.

To me our meeting felt propitious.
I hope it benefited her somehow—
—a moment of repose at least—
I hope she felt my reverence.
I like to think we helped each other
stay alive another day.

FERAL CAT

I see myself in the feral cat—
wary—but hungry enough
to be lured from the shadows
by a whiff of something good.
I put a dish of buttermilk
outside my open door
in hopes of wooing her
—eventually and gradually—
all the way inside.

She might never lose her fear
but I'll persist—I recognize
her need to stay reluctant
and afraid—her furtive ways
help her to survive—
the sustenance I offer
can't undo her history
but maybe it can help her
stay alive.

JENNIE'S GARDEN
Earth Day 2023

Today, forget-me-nots are blossoming.
A single lily—small, pale and delicate
but strong enough to rise up through
the cold hard ground—catches my eye
stops me in my tracks, drops me
to my knees and brings me face to face
with its reality, shows me there's a wider
wilder scheme of things where cottonwoods
exude their bittersweet perfume
and crows and jays begin again to build
their nests despite abundant evidence
that we are headed for the great collapse.
I for one am at a loss for what to do but
thank the sap for rising, thank the Earth
for her largesse, pay attention to the lily
and to fragile beauty everywhere, including
all of us who try our best to navigate despair,
to find our way to where the spirit blooms.

THE PRICE OF WINGS

I live in a valley of fog, cloud,
drizzle and damp, spanned
by a spectrum of gray—so
anything bright beguiles me.

This hunger for brilliance
is blessing and curse—
I get smitten by dazzlers,
fooled by the flash in the pan.

I might never outgrow it,
this yearning for light—
moth to the flame
the price of wings.

WHATEVER I SEE

Two brown horses graze in a pale winter field.
Crows alight on the bare arms of scrub oaks
flanking the barbwire fence.

A barn the color of old blood slumps groundward.
A pond reflects gray sky. A flock of tiny birds
flies in sudden unison from north to south.

Questions arise in my mind, then blow away.
Answers reside in the day as it is.
My teachers are whatever I see.

SUCH HAPPENINGS

A few leaves still cling to the grapevines,
pale yellow and trembling in cold wind.

This day belongs to such happenings—
seasons changing, awareness changing.

Meanwhile opinions fly like dark bullets.
The reality of winter settles in.

Shall we sit together by the fire
and make plans for spring?

CAPE BLANCO

Standing by the Sixes River
within view of the lighthouse,
on a trail leading to the beach,
my friends and I watched an osprey,
an eagle, and a hawk vie for dominion
of the sky above us.

The largest of the three—eagle—
swooped and screeched,
dodging the talons of osprey
and hawk, prevailing finally
as hawk veered inland and osprey
flew off toward the headland.

The river glistened as it flowed.
Time dilated, uttered an audible sigh.
The light surrounding us brightened,
clarified. The ground beneath us
was beating like a drum.

ANY CLUE
Wildfire Series IV
Cedar Creek Fire, September 2022

Crickets sang last night
until nearly dawn.
This morning's wind
blows from the east.

The creek runs low.
A cautious doe steps into view.
Crows chase other crows
across an ochre sky.

I wonder what this day
would have me do—
tea in hand, I go outside
in search of any clue.

Leaves are dropping,
letting go.
Tiny flakes of ash
drift down like snow.

REPORT FROM QUAANAAQ

Walls of ancient ice break off
then crash into the sea.

Rivulets of melting snow
sing eerie little melodies

    but never mind

that massive frozen place
is far, far away.

Still I wonder
what tunes did Nero play?

PLAYA SERIES XIX
contrails, cattails, sage

Alkali dust clouds rise,
billow, and dissipate
on the east shore
of Summer Lake.

A red-winged blackbird sings
its raspy flutelike song.
Swallows hunt the air
for what sustains.

Grasses bend down,
heavy-headed with seed.
Bees maraud the blossoms
of an old crabapple tree.

The pond reflects contrails,
cattails, and sage.
A mallard leaves
a widening V in its wake.

An eagle chases a hawk.
Tiny pollinators come,
lured by wildflowers.
The sky changes constantly.

If—as the pundits say—
these are degenerating times,
the Playa hasn't heard.

COYOTE AND BUDDHA
Cougar Creek Series LXV
   —for Jack

I sit awhile beside the spawning stream.
Eventually I stand to say goodbye—
to salmonberry, hemlock, cedar, fir,
and the lichen-covered Buddha resting
on a mossy log, placed there years ago
in memory of Jack.

The Buddha sits in deep repose,
rainwater in his upturned palms.
I follow his gaze—and there, not far
from his beatific smile—I see fresh scat!

I've been told Coyote doesn't live here anymore—
but what else could this be? I look closer,
see a little tooth, a tiny claw or two, some fur.
It seems Coyote swallowed a cat!

I step back, take a breath, and laugh—
a message from the wily one!
Coyote thrives, despite the damage
we have done!

HUNGRY ENOUGH

Six deer came to my yard this morning
and stood awhile in the cold rain.

A young doe, her belly beginning to swell
with next spring's fawn,

stepped into my garden to nibble
some yarrow, oregano, and rue,

hungry enough after days and nights of snow
to take what last summer she disdained.

Hunger can make a body do that—override
its preference for what is succulent and sweet—

bitter must do for now. Come June, that fawn
will taste the milk of wild intelligence.

DOWNHILL

Waking early to the sound of rain
still floating in a space where
memory of self dissolves,
my senses coalesce around
a fading dream as nighttime
slowly dovetails into dawn.

The creek outside my door runs loud
and high and fast and full. Rising up
through sleep I hear its downhill song:
   nothing is wrong
      nothing is wrong
         nothing is wrong

READY

One year into the plague
I went for a hike, up and up
through a young fir forest
then along a trail that led
to a wooden bridge.

Midway across, I stopped
to look down at the creek below—
fast-flowing, swollen and loud
with what sounded to me
like rapture.

But there I go—
anthropomorphizing again,
thinking the Earth is like I am—
relieved and delighted—after
a long dry season of dread.

But what do I know? Maybe
the Earth *is* like I am—or
better yet, maybe I am
like the Earth—burgeoning—
ready to feel the sap rising
one more time, ready to feel
the pure simple gladness
of Spring.

YACHATS
Series II

I don't know how to tell about
this morning's storm, but
the beach grass does—
lie flat against the dune
until the wind subsides.
Don't argue with the storm.
Bow down.

Gulls also know the way
to co-exist with what is real—
find a leeward place
and ride it out.

Those gulls who hunker down
know more than I about
the way to stay alive
when gale winds blow.
The beach grass too
is sentient in ways
beyond my human ken.
What is it I should know?

LIVING PROOF

Tethered by two linked strands
—a double helix, so they say—
I stay because my senses
hold me here, marry me
to this day—living proof
of Gaia's alchemy.

Bamboo windchimes clatter.
Grapes hang from a curling vine
—translucent, ripening.
A red tail hawk spirals high
and higher toward the sun.
Its shadow blends with mine.

WAITING FOR RAIN
Series III

I recognize myself
in the arid ground
the fading green

hear myself
in the thirsty crow
the creek

feel myself
in the hot wind
the fevered breeze

smell myself
in wildfire smoke
the burning fields

Some say I identify
too much with
what I see

I say—this kinship
helps me face
what facts reveal—

it's do or die—
time to learn
another way to be

FLASH OF HOURS

BREAK THE SPELL

Stuck in a web of my own weaving,
my spirit wanes—can I disentangle
from this mess I've made?
Can I save what's left of me
before the fading of the light?
Am I worth the fight?

Today I did my best to break the spell
of thoughts that sabotage the soul
but think I failed the test and now
there's nothing left for me to do but
go outside and feed the birds
and listen to the temple bell.

MY JOB THESE DAYS

My job these days is to study
the ways of quietude, to sit still
in whatever shade I can find,
let bygones be bygones,
pay heed to the day as it is,
recalibrate this tired old soul,
listen to the birds,
do least harm...

Pundits say the end is nigh—
debt ceiling about to fall and
we're doomed by rising tides
wildfire, politics...

Meanwhile I feel rebellion
light its little spirit-spark in me.
My weapon of choice is a song,
laughter my shield—I'm not sure
how to say what I feel but I'll try—
we're at the mercy of mystery,
wisdom gestating in darkness,
adrift in the animate real.

BOOTSTRAPS
Series II

My bootstraps are broken
after all these years of
being pulled up hard
and now I'm done—

done with wrangling,
done with wild rides—
nothing left to do but
hang up my spurs

and settle for another kind
of ride—one that carries me
away into a wilderness
no one lives to tell about.

BUCKET LIST

Mostly what I do these days
is try to lighten up, to free
my hands to do the job of
disentangling the many webs
I spent a lifetime weaving.

Once upon a time I worked
my fingers to the bone, making
what I hoped were treasures, but
today I sift the rubble, finding
junk and jewels in equal measure.

My bucket list is short:
  * Learn the language of birds.
  * Make amends.
  * Give it all away.
  * Die laughing.

MEMORY OF LIGHT

I woke up glad this morning
although nothing changed since
yesterday when I woke up sad—
same old body, same old mind,
but something shifted in my sleep—
did dreams recalibrate my sight?

This thing I call my self—
a walking question mark—
a pair of eyes, a pair of hands—
a baffled heart, a solitary
dancer in the dark.

One step forward, one step back
following a breadcrumb trail
through this realm of many moods—
left foot right foot left foot right—
lost but drawn toward the good
guided by the memory of light.

FLASH OF HOURS

It happened fast—
—this becoming old—
how could something as long
as this life be so fleeting?

This brilliant flash of hours
will be tomorrow soon enough.
Icy shadows will move and melt
and become yesterday.

If I look back
I drown in memory.
If I look ahead
I drown in what might be

—so here I am—
stuck in the moment at hand
where frost covers everything
and the morning glistens.

My mind's eye alights on the tropics
but the actual highway is closed—
fact is—we are snowbound
with nowhere to go.

I came with a plan but
the flow of seasons swept it away.
If nothing else after all these years
I have learned to defer to winter.

ANHEDONIA

In an ailing land colonized by fear
I live—like my neighbors do—
in peril of losing our birthright joy.

As a child I played hard and headlong,
my little companions running wild with me
through a landscape not yet scarred by war.

I still carry that spark of abandon
but it is buried deep, locked down,
waiting.

I make this poem because it wants me to.
Pleasure, so long overwhelmed by sadness,
hands me a match, whispers "strike anywhere."

HER HANDS

I was shopping for tea,
she for a pinch of spice—
two strangers at market
side by side, reaching
for the goods we sought.

Her face was private,
tender, kind. Her hands
looked aged and strong.
I wanted to say *your hands
are beautiful* but did not.

Instead I measured out
an ounce of dark Oolong
then as I stepped away
I saw her fill a little bag
with Saffron threads

and now this morning
I remember her—her face,
her lovely, sentient hands.
I sip my tea and ponder
what I might have said.

MORE THAN MEETS

The waxing gibbous moon
becomes more visible
as daylight fades
as dissipating clouds
move slowly
north to south
across a sky
whose color has
no human name.

This dream we're in
has taken everything
I own and now
there's nothing left
for me to do
but hit the road
for who knows where
and spread the word
that there is more
than meets the mortal eye
and we are here to learn
to love until we die.

HOW THE MOON MIGHT FEEL

Lately I feel how the moon might feel
if it felt anything at all—distant, cool,
held in place by the thinnest thread—
what the world wants: cycles, tides,
illumination.

Waxing, waning, harvest, blue, blood,
gibbous, full, new—I've seen them all
and now I'm done, ready to succumb
to gravity, to fade and fade until
there's nothing left of me but awe.

BIRTHDAY WISHES AT 77

To understand the phases of the moon
To learn the names of stars
To see light at the end of the tunnel
To write a page in the book of love
To do least harm
To mean what I say
To master the Australian Crawl
To laugh it off
To cut to the chase
To dive deep
To gather rosebuds while I may
To seek and find
To befriend the wolf at my door
To grow up
To make ends meet
To speak no evil
To render unto Caesar what is Caesar's
To blame no one

BURNING OLD JOURNALS

I fling old journals into the fire
sending my little confessions up
into the neutral night sky where
they'll dissipate as smoke and ash,
maybe join some wandering cloud
then someday fall, transmuted,
as beneficial rain.

> *all those righteous rants,*
> *those screeds, those*
> *words I wouldn't say*
> *out loud to anyone*

I light a match,
watch my petty grievances
flare up then disappear—
flash of heat, flame, light—
burnt offering—so many
sad old stories—tiny sparks
flying up bright as stars.

CROCUS

The prospect of dying brightens me—
strange, I suppose
but there it is—

not something I would say out loud
to anyone—but on this thin page
I can speak another way.

By brightens I mean heightens
the pleasure of being here,
somehow mitigates the pain.

Ice rain today—a minor surprise
in this time of extremes—meanwhile
the undaunted crocus thrives.

THESE DAYS

I've tried my best to make a home
here in this wilderness but lately
I begin to think my pioneering days
are numbered, and I wonder—
am I done with seeking, done
with waiting to be found?

These days my appetite is mainly
for surrender to the moment as it is—
no map, no guide, no plan, and I begin
to wonder if it's time to let what's left of me
be pulled away from here and carried off
to higher ground?

YOUR RIPENING

Because a shell protects an embryonic dove
and a shell protects a pearl, be patient
with your ripening.

Because the ground protects and hides a seed,
remember: darkness gestates possibility.

Because a chrysalis protects a butterfly,
because a veil conceals the lover's eye,
be patient with your ripening.

THIRST

I remember days and nights of early motherhood
—my baby's hungry cry causing milk to flow—
the sweet and mutual relief of give and take,
that necessary ritual every living being knows.

The gift of rain in drought is like that—the sky
pours out its burden, the ground receives,
its denizens revive, creeks and rivers swell
and sing again.

My children now have children of their own—
I gladly stand aside and watch them grow.
On the threshold of the open road
I feel a thirst I can't explain.

OLD FACE

Lines, so many, so deeply grooved,
each one rooted in its provenance—

worry, startle, shock, and awe
laughter, grief, delight, relief

every place I've ever been
everything I've seen and done,

everyone I've ever known or loved
and then released—

my face: a mirror of the world
as it reveals itself to me.

WHAT ELSE I CAN DO

Now that I'm invisible
and no one notices what I do,
I can get away with anything.
From behind these veils
of gray transparency
I can commit acts
of benign sabotage
like rocking the boat,
speaking out of turn,
and taking no for an answer.

Here's what else I can do
while no one sees:
look a gift horse in the mouth,
play with matches and fire,
take candy from strangers
and count my chickens
before they hatch.
I can stay up all night
writing poems by the light
of a candle burning at both ends.

FALLING

Since no one is there to hear,
a tree falls without a sound.
At least that's what they say.
Even so, I hear it in my mind,
that big old cedar crashing
as it crushes any upright thing
standing in its downward way.

> Meanwhile, unseen,
> I walk to the market
> for bread and wine.
> No one hears me go.

Old age has its benefits—
the pleasure of transparency,
the freedom of not being heard,
the rush that comes from yielding
to the pull of gravity at last,
the readiness to fall, invisible,
without a sound.

SOLSTICE

not ready to go
not eager to stay

what's left of me
hangs by a thread

I came empty handed
I'll leave the same way

sunlight caught
in a spider's web

ABOUT THE AUTHOR

Stacie Smith is a fourth-generation Oregonian living in her hometown, Eugene, Oregon, in the Willamette River Valley. This is her seventh book of poems.

Shanti Arts

Nature • Art • Spirit

Please visit us online
to browse our entire book catalog,
including poetry collections and fiction,
books on travel, nature, healing, art,
photography, and more.

Also take a look at our highly regarded art
and literary journal, *Still Point Arts Quarterly*,
which may be downloaded for free.

www.shantiarts.com